Reflections: Woods, Water, Life...

William D. Van Atta Jr.

Table of Contents

INTRODUCTION

Reflections is a collection of several true stories that have been a part of my life experience.

Boathouse Treasure was crafted from fond memories of my time living and working in the Canadian wilderness, and the treasure I found there.

La Cascada is an adventurous story that takes place in the mountains of the Dominican Republic during the late 1970s. It is a quest for gold.

I grew up during the Vietnam War. It was a turbulent time. **Capture the Flag** centers around events that happened on the school grounds during a war protest on the adjacent university campus.

I spent a good part of my early education at university-centered schools. For ninth grade, I had to move to a public school. **Frat Boy** takes place at this new school and allows the reader to experience a day in my life as a junior high student.

As in **Boathouse Treasure**, **Kakagi Ice Cream Express** also takes place in Canada. This time I am accompanied by some family members. In this story we enjoy a treat in the lakeside wilderness.

The Swim explores my life through swimming, from early childhood to adulthood and the present day. It reflects on these memories as I swim the Point to La Pointe 2.1 course from Bayfield, Wisconsin, to La Pointe, Wisconsin, on Madeline Island.

The last section of the book, **Poems**, is a sampling of poems I have written from grade school to the present day. They were written in good times and bad times, reflecting the ups and downs of daily life.

Thank you for reading. I hope you enjoy it.

Dedication

To all those who have guided me along the way. Family, friends, mentors and companion animals. To the forests and waters that have provided peace and comfort.

Acknowledgement

I would like to give special thanks to my mom, who introduced me to the poems of her grandfather, Joseph Russell Taylor and the author Robert W service. Thank you to the many teachers who patiently helped me with my deficient reading and writing skills.

For introducing me to the Canadian wilderness, I would like to thank the Whiteways—Dr. Robert (Red) and his wife, Marion. I worked my way through college as the Whiteways' handyman. And to my dad for the adventures I shared with him.

About the Author

William (Bill) D. Van Atta Jr. is a veteran Army aviator and retired registered nurse who is a native of the Midwest, now living in La Crescent, Minnesota. Bill holds a Bachelor of Science degree in geography from the University of Wisconsin–La Crosse.

After 12 years of service in the U.S. Army as both a rotary-wing and fixed-wing aviator, Bill went back to school. He graduated from The Norfolk General Hospital School of Nursing and then completed his Bachelor of Science in Nursing degree at Excelsior University and was licensed as an RN.

Bill practiced in several hospitals, including Level 1 and Level 2 trauma centers, where he specialized in the care of surgical, trauma, and burn patients.

When not writing, Bill enjoys spending time with his dogs. He especially likes being outdoors—camping, hiking, and photographing nature. Over the past couple of years, Bill has been putting his woodworking skills to the test building a small sailboat. He is an avid swimmer and has competed in several open water swimming competitions.

You can connect with Bill at: running_wolf57@yahoo.com

BOATHOUSE TREASURE

William D. Van Atta Jr.

Isn't it funny how the whisper of a word, a smell carried on the wind, the sound of an old familiar song, or simply a quick glance and touch of a cherished item can take you back to the past? I was cleaning my bedroom this morning when this happened, and I was taken back—back to a time long ago on a lake in Canada and the boathouse treasure.

All packed up, we settled into the baby blue VW Squareback and left La Crosse behind. It was late afternoon, and so began the eight-hour drive to Nestor Falls, Ontario, Canada. Behind the wheel to start the trip was Dr. Whiteway, also known as Red. Then there was me, riding shotgun. I was a college student working as the Whiteways' hired hand. Taking up the backseat was Nicholas, the Russian Wolfhound.

Driving nonstop through the late spring night, we travelled north, skirting the mighty Mississippi along the Great River Road towards the Twin Cities. We listened to Minnesota Public Radio as long as we could, and when we lost the signal, we tuned the dial to whatever we could find.

We made good time with Dr. Whiteway's lead foot, him ignoring the yellow and black placard placed on the dash by one of his kids. It read in bold black letters: "Slow Down."

As it got dark, Nick and I fell asleep. When I woke up, the Twin Cities were far behind, and we were in northern Minnesota nearing the Canadian border. The night sky was taking on the pinkish glow of morning. More and more lakes started to fill the landscape, and a scent of pine lingered in the air.

We arrived at International Falls, stopped for gas and a few dry goods, then meandered our way through town to the border crossing. Our time to get through Canadian customs was brief. Just a few questions, a quick inspection, and a friendly pat on Nick's head, and we were official. We passed the "Welcome to Canada" sign and moved on.

Now clear of the border and Fort Frances, we started to get excited, for the lake was but an hour away. This last hour of the drive always seemed to be the longest. We continued north, Lake of the Woods not far off to the west and Rainy Lake to the east. Nick poked his head out the window, taking in the new smells. He wagged his tail with approval.

We weaved through the forest, past a seaplane base, then took a right turn onto the gravel road that opened to Kakagi Lake and Hanson's Hideaway Lodge.

I was always awestruck as Kakagi's magical beauty was revealed before my eyes: the deep blue waters, rocky shoreline, magnificent forests, and the puffy white clouds. We unloaded our gear, then started our walk to the camp store. Looking back at the dock, we could see the boat was already in the water waiting for us.

Entering the store, we found Ken Hanson stocking some goods. Ken and Dr. Whiteway greeted each other, then struck up a conversation. As they talked, I looked around the store, eyeing some things I could take home and give as gifts. I overheard Dr. Whiteway ask Ken if the lake water was still safe to drink, and Ken replied that it was.

We gathered up a few items: fresh bread, some preserves, a slab of uncut bacon, and some fresh linens for the lodge. Saying goodbye to Ken, we headed for the boat.

We quickly loaded up, started the boat's twin Evinrude outboards, and with Dr. Whiteway at the helm, headed eastward to the far side of the lake. The lake was tame this morning, making for a dry, comfortable ride.

As we glided across the water, I reminisced about the previous year at the lake. That summer, we fell several pines, stripped their bark, and set them up for drying. One of the guests that year was the son of one of the Whiteways' friends in Chicago.

When we had free time, he'd take the aluminum skiff out, terrorizing the quiet waters while racing about the bays, blaring Neil Diamond songs from his boombox. I enjoy a Neil Diamond tune but not in the Canadian wilderness. Here, I enjoy the many sounds and songs you hear when tuned to nature. To this day, "Cracklin' Rosie" takes me back to those days.

This year, there was no boy from Chicago, no boombox, no Neil Diamond.

Dr. Whiteway navigated the boat through the waters, passing by several islands and avoiding the shallows that lay hidden beneath the lake. We rounded one last island, and the dock at the Whiteways' Kakagi Lodge, with its welcoming Canadian flag, came into view. The boat slowed, and we drifted to the dock.

The lodge, built in the 1930s, was resurrected from years of abandonment and now, with its subdued green siding, sat proudly looking west across the lake. A couple of families shared the lodge. It was now Dr. Whiteway's turn to enjoy some time there.

The great room, a focal point of the dwelling, had a large stone fireplace with a huge bull moose head above it. In the afternoon, the moose was illuminated as light shone through the west-facing dormer across from it. There was a large screened porch off the great room where you could watch the beautiful sunsets while gently swinging on the porch swing.

There was no running water, no electricity, and no generator. Water was brought to the lodge from the lake in galvanized steel pails. Bathing was done in the lake. The kitchen did have a propane-fueled stove and refrigerator.

This would be my second time at the lake helping the Whiteways with the construction of their personal log cabin on the grounds. This year, we were starting on the construction of the foundation and subflooring. We were the first to arrive at the lodge, so we had to open things up and prepare it for the season. This included removing locks, stocking the refrigerator and pantry, hooking up the propane for the stove and refrigerator, and lastly picking the rooms we would sleep in, then unpacking and making beds.

By the time we finished, most of the day was gone. We cooked up a quick dinner, then sat on the porch to watch the sunset. We were all quite tired. We lit the lanterns as it became dark, then headed for our rooms. Tomorrow we would resume the construction of the new cabin.

The dawn broke, the loons started laughing, and rays of soft light filtered through the cobweb-decorated windows. I could hear tiny feet outside walking across the roof—maybe squirrels or crows? Wiping the sleep from my eyes, I rolled out of my warm bed and met the chilly morning air. As I got dressed, I could smell breakfast cooking. I followed my nose up to the kitchen where I enjoyed some eggs, bacon, and toast with Dr. Whiteway and Nick.

After cleaning up from breakfast, we headed outside to inspect the logs we cut the previous year. All the logs looked good.

We then proceeded to the building site. The planned site had a northwestern view of the water on a rock outcropping that sloped toward the shoreline.

We worked clearing loose debris from the cabin footprint, marked out the footing locations, and then took a break for lunch and an afternoon bath and swim.

I put on my swimsuit and gathered up some soap. We used Ivory soap because it floats. I also picked up a towel and shampoo—yes, I had hair back then.

Taking a bath in frigid Kakagi was a simple task once you got the nerve to jump in. To start, you took the jump, then quickly climbed out, lathered up, and jumped back in for the rinse. If you were brave, you would swim around for a while, then climb out as you were getting numb or when visions of Sam McGee and the "Alice May" appeared.[1]

On some days, after working up a sweat, I would climb the ladder to the boathouse roof and take the ten-foot plunge to the waters below. It was from the roof the previous year that I first saw the old sunken boat on the lake bottom a few yards from the boathouse entrance. I believe it was a Chris-Craft runabout with an inboard engine.

The story told was that years ago it caught fire, burned to the waterline, and sank. There were some black-and-white photos of the boat during its early days on the lake. They hung on the wall in the lodge with other pictures from the past. This year, I brought my dive mask, fins, and snorkel and planned to take a closer look at the wreck.

Now all dried off, warmed up, and dressed, I went back up the path to the lodge for some relaxation and a snack.

Working at the lodge was generally easygoing. We worked every day but always took time to relax and enjoy the beautiful surroundings.

---

[1] Sam McGee and the "Alice May", are mentioned in the poem, The Cremation of Sam McGee, by Robert W. Service

The next task at the building site was to build up the foundation on the rocky ground. This involved drilling rebar into the rock and constructing concrete piers. We had to make our own concrete, which meant taking a trip to Sand Island. We chose a nice day for the trip to the island. We loaded the boat with some large buckets, a shovel, and a screen for cleaning debris from the sand. Climbing aboard, we shoved off the dock and headed north to find the island's hidden sandy beach.

After a 20-minute ride, we found the island and beached the boat. There was a coarse grinding sound as the boat rubbed against the sandy bottom. We climbed over the side and helped Nick out of the boat. While he sniffed around, we got organized to collect the sand we would use for the concrete mix. Shoveling away, we scooped up the coarse sand, sifting it through the screen into the buckets. We continued scooping and sifting for an hour or two as Nick supervised from the tree line.

Once we had enough sand, we all climbed back in the boat, fired up the motors, and headed back to the lodge.

We continued our work on the cabin, and it was coming along nicely. We drilled the rock and built up piers that the floor support beams would rest on.

Some days I would spend my free time canoeing about the lake. One day I headed out in the early evening so I could take some sunset pictures. On my way, I stopped at the island just west of the lodge and dumped a collection of compost on a rock near the water's edge. The crows would congregate on the rock and noisily eat up whatever goodies they could find.

Kakagi in Ojibway is translated as black bird, so the lake also became known as Crow Lake.

I got back to paddling again and found a good spot to take some shots of the sunset. I set my tripod up in some shallow water, mounted the camera, and waited for the magic.

The sunset was starting to take place. I began shooting. The shutter clicked away as the sun began its descent toward the horizon. The colors started out a pale yellow, then progressed to pink, orange, and finally a fiery red that was reflected in the still waters. The colors faded, and darkness was not far behind.

I gathered up my gear, climbed back into the canoe, and started the race back to the boathouse. It was a race for sure—a race against the gathering swarm of hungry mosquitoes. I paddled faster and faster, and the black cloud chasing me grew larger and darker.

I managed to beat them to the boathouse but lost time tying up the canoe. Without warning, the bloodsuckers were upon my skin, and I started my sprint to the safe haven of the lodge. There, I took shelter behind the slamming screen door.

To avoid night bites from any stray mosquitoes that made it inside, we would shut the windows and doors and spray insecticide throughout the bedrooms. Looking back, this was probably not a good idea. At least we got to sleep peacefully.

.

The long Canadian days seemed to pass by too quickly, and my time at Kakagi would soon be over. Still, I hadn't gotten a close look at the sunken boat. One afternoon, after nailing some floor joists, I suited up, grabbed my snorkeling gear, and headed down to the boathouse for some wreck diving.

The water was a little warmer than a few weeks ago, but it was still cold. I had a neoprene vest that helped somewhat with the cool water. I donned my gear and jumped in. I swam out, soon found the boat, and started my dive to the bottom to check it out. The wreck was in about ten feet of water.

Holding my breath for as long as I could, I surveyed it from stern to bow. I came up for air, then went down again. I was hoping to find some souvenirs or salvageable items. There wasn't much left of the craft except for the engine and some of the boat's hull. I took one last breath and swam down. This time, I went to the stern and looked underneath. I found the rudder and a large brass propeller half buried in the mud. I surfaced, caught my breath, and decided to call it a day.

That night, lying in bed, I thought about the brass propeller and came up with a plan.

In the morning, over breakfast, I told Dr. Whiteway about my dive on the old boat and my idea—my plan to remove the propeller from the wreck. He listened intently and gave his approval. That afternoon, after work, I began my salvage operation.

This time, wrench in hand, I dove to the bottom of the boat. It took several dives to adjust the wrench to fit the nut that secured the propeller. With a final adjustment, I dove to the propeller, placed the wrench on the nut, and pulled with all my strength. The nut didn't budge. I made several dives to try to remove the nut with no luck. It was time for another plan.

I decided that the only option was to cut the propeller free, but that would have to wait until tomorrow. I updated Dr. Whiteway, and he was able to locate a hacksaw among several tools in the utility room.

That afternoon, I returned to the wreck and, saw in hand, started cutting away the nut. Dive after dive, I held my breath, sawing away at the nut until it finally fell away. I returned to the surface and rested for a while.

I caught my breath, then returned to the bottom to remove the prop from the shaft. I pulled and pulled, but the old boat refused to give up its propeller. I even tried pounding it free with no luck. It was then that I decided to cut the drive shaft where it exited the hull.

Obsessed and determined, I returned to the bottom again and again until the saw blade made it through the inch-and-a-half-thick steel shaft. I floated to the surface, exhausted, and rested on my back. I made one last dive to the bottom to grab the propeller and shaft and bring it to the surface.

Cradling it in my arms, I swam with it to the boathouse dock and removed it from the water. As I climbed onto the dock, Dr. Whiteway came down the path. We both grinned as we closely inspected the treasure.

My days at Kakagi were coming to an end. We were able to finish up the subfloor on the cabin and place a couple of logs, and then it was time to listen to the crying loons while watching one last sunset.

In the morning, we would turn the lodge over to another family, then return south.

I dusted off the old propeller and placed it back in a corner of my bedroom. Seeing it and touching it had taken me back to the lake, to the boathouse, and to the sunken treasure I found there many years ago.

It was then that I came to realize that the treasure wasn't the old boat's propeller at all, but the many cherished memories I had of my days in the Canadian wilderness on a lake named Kakagi.

Prologue

I never got to see the completed cabin. My life, careers, and new adventures consumed my time. Still, I think of my days in Canada and see a trip north in the future.

The reference to "Sam McGee" and the "Alice May" in the story is from a poem written by Robert W. Service, The Cremation of Sam McGee. It is one of my favorites.

KAKAGI LODGE
NESTOR FALLS
ONTARIO

La Cascada

William D. Van Atta Jr.

Within a matter of hours, we had leapfrogged south, leaving the sub-zero February cold of La Crosse, Wisconsin, for the warm tropics of the Dominican Republic. We spent the night at El Embajador Hotel in Santo Domingo, and now Dick Keller's King Air, loaded with scuba gear and anxious adventurers, left the ground and headed north for the town of Mao.

Flying the plane was Dick, owner of Keller Rock and Lime. I believe he said he was a crew member on a B-17 bomber in World War II. In the seat to the right of Dick sat an old Black man, Bill Richards. Bill, a native of the Dominican Republic, had recently returned to the country. He was a mining superintendent before he left years ago during the revolution, fearing for his life.

In the seat behind Dick was Dean Phillips, owner of a gas company in Iowa. From what we were told, his business took him from rags to riches. Dean picked us up in his Cessna twin-engine airplane two days ago in La Crosse and flew us to his home in Iowa, which had a private airstrip. After landing and sliding down the snow-covered runway, he taxied the plane to the hangar next to his home, where we spent the first night.

In the back of the plane, among the scuba tanks, picks, shovels, and black plastic sampling bags, sat my dad, Dr. William Van Atta Sr., a college professor, and myself, William Jr., a college student and amateur photographer. My dad, a master dive instructor, and I were asked by Jim Silvy, owner of another gas company, to take bottom samples from a small pool in the Cordillera Central Mountains. The pool was fed by a 300-foot vertical falls known as Salto de Jicomé. This waterfall is one of the highest in the country.

There was gold in the pool and along the river, but Silvy and his friends wanted to know if there was enough to make mining profitable. We were told that the river and pool were panned and worked previously with some success. It is believed that the ancient native people took gold from the river before the invasion of the Spaniards. It was rumored that the spirit of a chief haunted the falls.

During the early 1950s, an American had taken gold from the pool, but his equipment was destroyed by floods, and he left the country.

Jim was in a second plane, along with Mort Walker, a wheat farmer with 10,000 acres in Australia. Also onboard was Merlin Savage, who told us he was a bodyguard to General Douglas MacArthur in WWII. Merlin had recently arranged a large oil deal between Kuwait and the Dominican Republic. The remaining passengers were a mechanical engineer, a doctor, and our host, Ron Ortez, Treasurer of Santo Domingo. Ron met us on arrival to the country and used his connections to whisk us through the airport, bypassing customs.

We were almost there. Dick and Mort were on the lookout for the tiny field on which we were to land. They didn't look long when a crop duster appeared, flew up, and guided us onto the landing strip.

We were soon on the ground, unloading all the equipment needed for our trip to the falls. There were many people watching and helping. A small building stood at the edge of the field. In front of it were two armed soldiers. A gold Ford LTD was parked just inside the building. We soon learned that the car belonged to the provincial general, General Oliverez. The car was a gift from President Balaguer. The general met us at the airfield, and we all shook his hand while his bodyguards watched closely.

After some friendly chatting, we climbed into three cars and sped down the rough gravel road toward town. Along the road were several laborers working in large green fields of rice and tobacco.

We bounced off the gravel onto the blacktop of Mao and pulled up to the Hotel Cahoba. The General's car arrived first. In the entrance of the hotel, I could see his bodyguards dressed in camouflaged jungle fatigues, checking the area. They both had automatic weapons. One had a Thompson submachine gun, and the other had an Israeli-made Uzi machine pistol. They looked at my dad and me with suspicion.

When we were all in the lobby, we checked in, then headed for the dining room and lunch. After eating, we retired to our rooms for showers and a nap.

It was getting dark as Dad and I emerged from our room. We walked out to the patio, where Ron, Bill, and some of the others were enjoying drinks in the tropical air. Adjacent to the patio was the swimming pool, which was half-filled with greenish water. The patio and pool were surrounded by a rock wall with jagged pieces of colored glass embedded in the top, serving as a barrier for trespassers.

The waiter went to get me a Coke and my dad a beer. As he returned, the General's car rolled into the drive. His guards checked the area, and then the General and all the investors entered for a conference in a small room next to the pool.

Within five minutes, they reemerged, then left the hotel with the General in two waiting cars. Bill told us that the General had invited them to his house. They had evidently asked the General to join their group. This was necessary if they wished to be active in his province.

Gold was only a secondary reason for the investors' interest in the Dominican Republic. Their primary interest was in the purchase of an undeveloped oceanside resort in Samina. It was during an earlier trip related to the resort that they learned of the gold and decided to check it out. Because some of the men had not seen the resort yet, they decided to look it over before returning home.

Bill, the engineer, my dad, and I had not been alone long when the gold LTD reappeared in the driveway. The General's two bodyguards emerged and approached us. They talked with Bill, and then he translated for us. He said we were all to go to the General's home.

We all got up and went to the car. As I sat down in the back seat, I saw the machine pistol belonging to a guard lying on the floor between my legs. He retrieved it, then sat down in the front seat next to the driver. The driver slammed his door and accelerated down the driveway onto the dark road. He drove wildly down the narrow streets and stopped in front of a darkened three-story, flat-topped building.

The guard and driver stepped from the car. They told us to wait, then walked across the street into the dark stairwell. After a few moments, one of them returned to lead us up the stairs. The guard walked in front of us with weapon in hand to check the flights of stairs ahead. We had to stop at each floor while he checked ahead. We passed the third floor and stepped onto the roof.

Jim, Dick, and the others were all there, relaxing with drinks in hand. After about an hour of talking, drinking, and planning, it was time to leave. Two of the General's men drove four of us back to the hotel and then later returned with the others. We then walked into town for some dinner.

After dinner, we returned to the hotel for some much-needed sleep. Tomorrow at 5:00 AM, we would leave for the waterfall. We were told it was only a short distance; however, it would take several hours to get there on the mountain roads and paths.

With thoughts of the past day's activity, I drifted off into a deep sleep, not knowing that tomorrow's trip to the waterfall would be one of the most interesting and adventurous days of the trip—and of my life.

At 5:00 AM, the phone rang, ending our rest. My dad and I climbed out of our beds, got dressed, then headed to the dining room for a quick breakfast. It was not long before several four-wheel drive vehicles arrived to transport us to the waterfall.

Dawn was just breaking when we finally got loaded up and started our journey. My dad and I rode in the back of a green Toyota Jeep. The caravan traveled down the paved road, then after a few miles veered right onto a very rough dirt road. We held on and felt every bump shaking our bones.

We had not gone far when we came to a halt. The road ahead was underwater and appeared to be impassable. We exited the Jeep and walked along the dry ground while the drivers, one by one, took a try at driving through the mud. One vehicle got stuck and had to be pulled free.

Now clear of the muddy obstacle, we climbed back into the vehicles and continued down the winding backroads. After what seemed like hours, we arrived at the river, only to find that the bridge crossing had been washed out.

Within a few minutes, we were loading a small ferry that crossed the river adjacent to the bridge. A rope was strung across the water and anchored to trees on either side. The boat was pulled across the river by the boat's operator.

We climbed aboard the ferry, and after several trips, everyone and all the equipment made it to the other side.

The rest of the trek would be on foot. Burros carried all our equipment. Our escorts for this part of the journey were two armed soldiers.

It was now time to start the hike to the waterfall. The trail was close to the river and passed many small farms. There were people of all ages along the trail. They always gave a friendly wave as we walked along.

The trail slowly got steeper and narrower, and some of the out-of-shape businessmen started to struggle. The local guides fashioned some walking sticks for us to help on the uneven terrain. We took several breaks, stopping at a few farms where we would rest.

At one farm, the soldiers picked some wild mangos. They cut them up and shared them with the group. I had never eaten or even known about mangos. I took a bite of the juicy fruit and found it quite refreshing.

Soon the break was over, and we were back on the never-ending trail. We found ourselves crossing the river several times and then followed it the remainder of the way to the falls.

We had been walking for three or four hours now, and everyone was getting tired. We were all ill-prepared for the excursion. Some of the men were dressed in casual business attire and street shoes. One was even wearing a leather jacket and cowboy boots. We carried no water, no food, and only had the clothes on our backs.

Soon, the parade of Americans came to a halt. A soldier came from up ahead and told us we were close. He pointed up the trail, shouting, "La Cascada! La Cascada!"

In the distance, we could hear the low rumble of Salto De Jicome's cascading waters. As we moved forward, we could feel the cool, misty breath of the falls. Occasionally, we could look up and see it through breaks in the forest canopy.

We emerged from the vegetation, and there it was—the magnificent waterfall. You couldn't capture the beauty of the falls in a single glance. You had to scan it, looking up and down. As if alive, the water danced its way down the rock face to the pool below. Wisps of windblown mist were cast through the air, dropping the temperature considerably. We all stood and watched for several minutes, hypnotized by its spirit.

It was now getting late, and we had to get to work sampling the pool. We quickly unpacked the burros and set up our gear on the beach near the pool.

Everyone gathered to brief on the plan for collecting the samples. After the brief, my dad and I suited up and prepared to enter the water.

14

I stepped into the pool first. I was tethered to a line that my dad tended. We used the line for safety and as a guide to help us decide where to take a sample. We alternated between diving and tending. We worked our way around the circumference of the pool, taking samples every 10 feet. We finished in a couple of hours with about 60 samples. The samples were about one gallon each and placed into black garbage bags.

By the time we left the water and changed out of our gear, it was early evening, and we were falling under the shadow of the mountain. As it started to get dark, it was decided that it was best to remain at the falls until morning instead of risking travel at night.

The mountain air grew cooler, and then one of the guides got a fire going. Word of our presence traveled fast, and soon some of the local people showed up with chicken and rice to share with us. It was a welcoming treat for our hungry bellies.

With our bellies full, we started to think about sleep. We had no sleeping bags and no blankets. Our dilemma was trying to figure out how to sleep and stay warm. After considering our limited options, we decided the only thing to do was to make use of the black garbage bags we had. It was then that we decided to use the bags as sleeping bags. Yes, we ended up sleeping in garbage bags.

It was a long night. Needless to say, the black plastic garbage bags provided no warmth. They did provide some protection from the damp, misty air of the falls. The night passed slowly. At first light, I awoke cold and in the fetal position. One by one, we emerged from the black bags and made our way to the fire. I don't recall if there was anything to eat, but there was coffee that one of the guides made. It was mixed with honey and passed around in an old bottle. I slowly warmed up in the sunshine and prepared for the return trip.

For the trip back, we broke into two groups. One group would go with the burros, all the equipment, and the samples on the trail that brought us in. The second group would go back by way of the upper falls. This route would involve some steep, slippery climbing. My dad and I were in this group along with Jim, Dean, Ron, a soldier, and a guide.

We got underway and started our climb up the muddy hillside to the left of the falls. We watched as the other group started their return down the trail. Grabbing hold of vegetation, we pulled ourselves hand over hand up the side of the waterfall until we reached the top. We rested and took in the view of the valley below.

Up top, we saw evidence of some small concrete dams and shoots aimed at redirecting the water flow. These were probably built by the American who worked the area years ago. Continuing up the river, we walked until joining the trail that would take us to the vehicles and the comfort of the hotel.

This new route took us across the high ground. We continued to come upon many small farms and friendly people.

Occasionally we could see the river and its rapids in the valley below.

After a couple of hours of walking, we made it to the waiting vehicles. Within a few minutes, the other group arrived. They rode the ferry across the river to join us.

All loaded up, we took our seats and drove back to Mao. At the hotel, we got cleaned up, had a quick lunch, checked out, and then headed back to the airfield.

Everything was routine from here. We flew back to Santo Domingo. Then, after a night of rest, we flew back to La Crosse and the cold of winter.

A few weeks passed, and then my dad learned from Jim that the lab found gold in the samples we collected, but there was not enough to make it profitable for a full-scale mining operation. I guess you could say that this was a victory for the spirit of La Cascada.

I found it a struggle to get back into the routine of my studies. I would often catch myself daydreaming about the adventure I shared with my dad. Even today, after nearly 50 years, the spirit of the falls touches me, taking me back to the Dominican Republic and La Cascada!

Capture the Flag

William D. Van Atta Jr.

Just another day in God's country for a 12-year-old boy or so it seemed. It was a brisk spring day in late May 1970, still half asleep, l was up getting ready for school. For breakfast, a piece of peanut butter, and jelly toast and a glass of orange juice. Then off to school on my one speed Schwinn bicycle.

I was a student at the Campus School on the grounds of the University of Wisconsin -La Crosse. The school, grades K through 9, occupied what is now Morris Hall on the southwest side of the campus.

I lived about 3 blocks from the school, so the bike ride was a short one. North on 17th Place to Main, then a left turn, right turn, another left on State Street and there I was. I secured my bike in the bike rack among the assortment of bicycles one of them a beautiful new five speed stingray with a banana seat and high-rise handlebars. I eyed the bike then scurried into the school.

I don't remember what grade I was in, but I guess I could figure it out if I strained my brain enough. I do however remember the day very well, sometimes with mixed feelings especially knowing more about what led to the events influencing the day.

MAY
1970

S	M	T	W	T	F	S
				1	2	3	4
5	6	7	8	9	10	11
12	13	14	15	16	17	18
19	20	21	22	23	24	25
26	27	28	29	30	31	

Sitting at my desk daydreaming I was awakened by the bell. The school day began, as always, standing, hand on heart facing the flag and reciting the pledge of allegiance.

I never really liked school I just figured it was another part of life that one had to endure. The day was progressing slowly. We trudged through one subject after another until it was time for a few minutes on the playground.

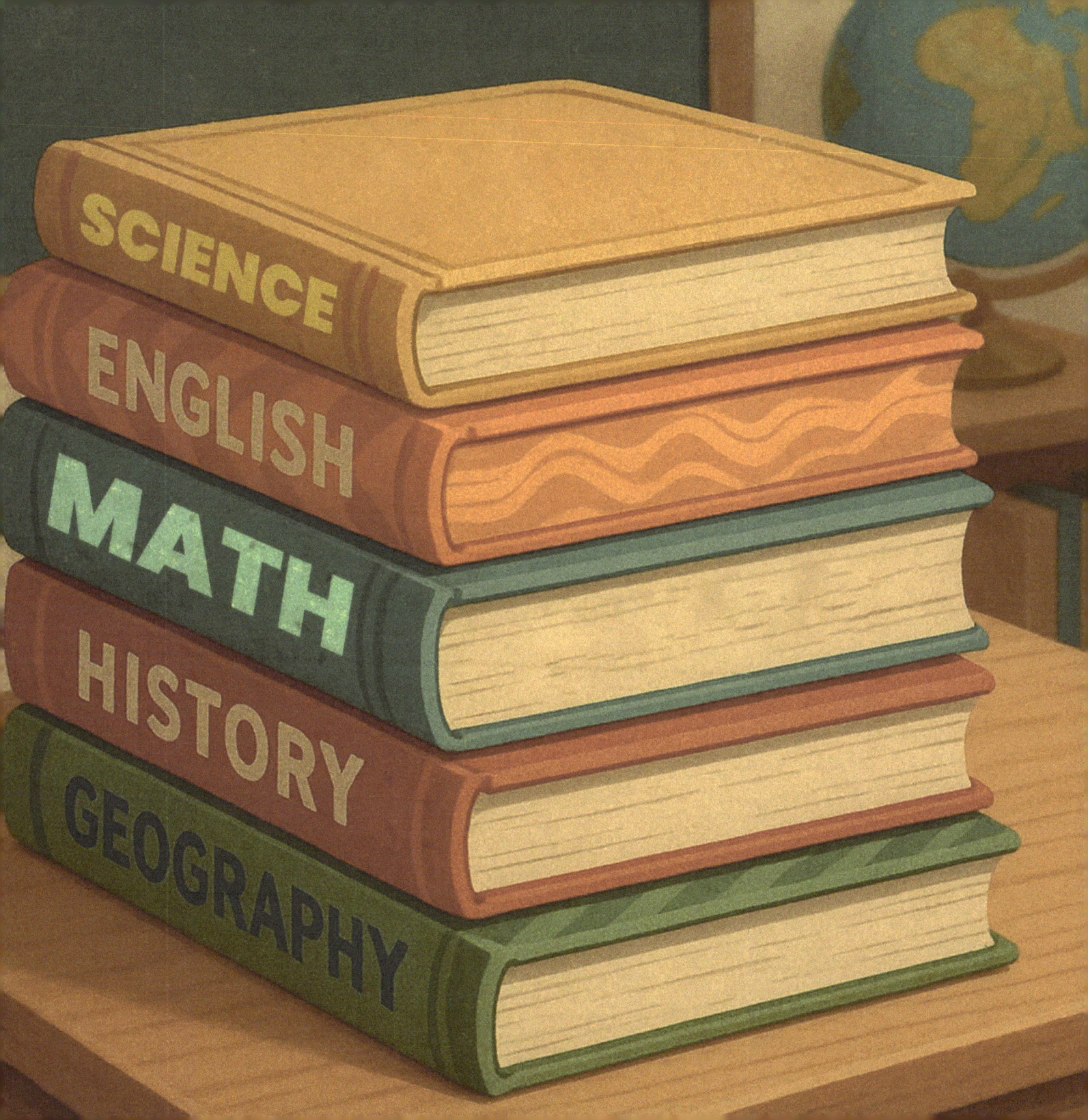

We paraded down the stairs in orderly fashion and out the doors, then we ran like crazy to the playground for a game of kickball. It was then that we noticed something was different. Several college students had left class and were protesting the war. I still have the image in my head of one protester whose dog had a peace sign shaved into its fur and highlighted with florescent pink paint. The protesters were noisy but peaceful and didn't interrupt our game.

Game over, recess done, we filed back through the doors, up the stairs and into the classroom. The day went by, science, math, lunch, music and then down to the lower level where the art room was.

The art teacher was a free spirit, and she always had some interesting projects for us. There was always music playing, Simon and Garfunkel, Chicago, The Beetles and other popular artists from the day, DJ'd by a couple of classmates. The art room had the smell of turpentine and oil paint lingering in the air. There were pieces of student's artwork hanging on the walls.

The lower level of the school was partially below ground, with big windows that looked out onto the large field in the front of the school. While standing you had a view of the grounds outside. We were working away at our projects listening to "Bridge Over Troubled Water" when we heard things picking up outside. We crowded in front of the windows and standing on tiptoes could see the protesting crowd growing. They were chanting and shouting many of them waving signs. We remained calm but interested in what was going on outside our school. Slowly the crowd approached the flagpole near the front of the school. A couple of long-haired shirtless guys reached the pole, grabbed the halyard and started lowering the flag to half staff. Once at half staff they stepped back and joined the crowd with its chanting, yelling and sign waving.

It was then that something stirred in us, a sort of awakening or calling. Without hesitation or prompting several of us left the art room went up the stairs and outside. We proceeded toward the flagpole through the chaos of the crowd and stopped in front of our school's flag. We fumbled with the halyard then pulled the flag back to full staff. As if in a game, we had captured the flag. We stood in anticipation of some sort of retaliation but there was none. Instead, the crowd fell silent and bowed their heads in prayer. Shameless, we went back inside to art class to work on our projects and listen to music.

The day went on as usual, and the flag remained flying high above our proud school. Soon the bell rang. The day of learning was over.

Once again, I was on my bike, pedaling home.

I never really thought about that day till years later after the truth of that period had been sorted out. Right or wrong we were just kids influenced by the adults and environment in our world. We were doing what we thought needed to be done when we captured the flag.

Frat Boy

William D. Van Atta Jr.

Ninth grade, Lincoln Junior High, La Crosse, Wisconsin. This was the first public school I attended, so it was a new experience for me, humbling and a bit traumatic. I experienced everything from having my bike stolen from the bike rack to being spit on in the hallway.

I did pride myself on being a standout athlete, but at best, I was just a very shy, mediocre student. Being an athlete, I was good in gym where I excelled, always ready to give one hundred percent.

The gym teacher was affectionately known as Mr. D because no one could pronounce his long Italian last name. He was a short, stout, dark-haired man fitted with dark-rimmed glasses. He was very loud and outspoken.

His office was next to the locker room. Behind his desk, he proudly displayed some memorabilia from his past. Centered on the wall and flanked by framed photos, diplomas, and certificates of achievement hung what appeared to be a fraternity paddle. The handle sported a leather strap; Greek letters were painted on the grip, and carved into the paddle were raised waffles.

I don't recall the time of year this story took place, but by my best guess, it was early spring.

The school day started off as usual. I spent the first period at Central High School, where five of us took Geometry. We were then bussed to Lincoln for study hall, Spanish, Biology, English, Civics, Art, and Gym.

As usual, the day dragged on with nothing out of the ordinary except for my struggle to stay awake. Then, before I knew it, it was time for gym. The bell rang. I closed the cover on "The Merchant of Venice" and, with my classmates, left English behind. We all filled the hallway and moved on to the next class.

I meandered through the corridors, then through the lunchroom with its blue-green tiles. Random student art decorated the walls, and there was a lingering odor of institutional food in the air.

Clear of the lunchroom, I took a right to the hallway leading to the gym and locker rooms. As I approached the gym, I could hear laughter and horseplay. I stepped through the door and into the gym. Before me was near-total chaos. Kids were running around the gym in their street shoes, and Mr. D was nowhere to be found. His office and locker room doors were locked. Instead of joining the chaos, I sat with a few other boys in the bleachers and watched the commotion.

Several minutes passed, and still no Mr. D. Then, without warning, he angrily appeared in the gym doorway. He stepped across the threshold and, in a loud drill sergeant voice, barked out for everyone to stop and line up on the end line, except for those in the bleachers.

It was library quiet. He walked up and down the line, lecturing the nervous boys about their behavior and their violation of the sacred rule to stay off the yacht-varnished gym floor with street shoes.

Mr. D then turned around and marched to his office. He fumbled with his assortment of keys. Finding the right one, he unlocked his office and went in. He soon emerged, and in his right hand, wielded what appeared to be the fraternity paddle that he displayed on his office wall. Mr. D walked back towards the lined-up boys, clapping the paddle against his open hand as he went along. Like a drumbeat, it echoed in the quiet gym. His black-striped, white gym shoes squeaked on the shiny floor as he came to a halt in front of the boys.

He ordered the guilty to bend over and grab their ankles. Walking behind the boys, he continued down the line, and one by one, like a henchman, rendered punishment. The paddle was swung with force and slapped against each awaiting bottom; it gave a loud pop as each boy rocked forward from the impact of the blow. This was often followed by a grunt or moan. There was no crying, but I did notice a few tears. Those of us in the bleachers watched and listened in disbelief, quietly thankful we did not have to take part in this activity.

Mr. D rendered the last blow, then ordered everyone back to the bleachers. In embarrassment and shame, the punished settled into the benches where we all sat quietly for the rest of class.

The bell rang, breaking the silence. We all got up and, in an orderly fashion, left the gym. I only had one period left, study hall, where I could get most of my homework done. Then, as quickly as my day began, school was out.

I walked outside to the bike rack. Today, my trusty bike was still there. I unlocked it, climbed on, and pedaled home.

I'm not sure if I told my mom and dad about that school day, but I imagine school administration found out about the paddling that Mr. D inflicted. I think that if this happened today, the corrective action taken would be harsh.

KAKAGI ICE CREAM EXPRESS

William D. Van Atta Jr.

It was a warm August day at Kakagi Lake in Ontario, Canada, and we were looking for some relief and a treat. With a treat in mind, we made our way to the boathouse and climbed aboard the small boat tied up to the dock. The boat, made of wood, appeared to be quite old. Its red hull was fading now from years of trusty use. It got its propulsion from a small Mercury outboard motor of 15 horsepower. I primed the motor, made a few pulls on the starter cord, and the motor sputtered, then fired up, engulfing us in a white cloud of exhaust smoke and the smell of gasoline.

With a gentle twist on the throttle, the boat lunged forward, and we began our journey across the lake. My sister Molly and I were on a mission. Our task was to obtain a gallon of vanilla ice cream for the hot fudge sauce I would cook up for the evening dessert. We bounced about the boat as we entered the open water, navigating our way around numerous islands and carefully avoiding the rocky hazards that lay hidden below Kakagi's waves.

After 30 minutes of wind and spray, we approached our destination. I throttled the motor back to a gentle rumble and coasted to the dock. We were now at Hanson's Hideaway Lodge. We strolled up the dock and up the hill to the lodge store. Entering the store, the squeaky screen door slammed shut behind us. At the counter, we found Ellen Hanson. We greeted each other and talked a bit, then made our way to the freezer. Molly opened the chest, reached through a frosty cloud, and pulled out a gallon of vanilla ice cream. We were on the clock now, as we had to make it back before our icy treat completely melted.

With the carton secured in a styrofoam cooler and the bill paid, we scrambled to the boat and headed back across the choppy lake. We were making good time on our ride to the Whiteways' Kakagi Wilderness Lodge, where my mom, dad, Molly, and I were guests. Our hosts were Dr. (Red) and Mrs. (Marion) Whiteway.

The lodge, within viewing distance of the lake, was accessible only by boat and had been in Mrs. Whiteway's family since the 1930s. It had become forgotten and neglected over the years until it was brought to life again in the 1960s. There was no electricity or plumbing. Water was hauled in pails from the lake, and bathing was done in Kakagi's frigid waters. It did, however, have the convenience of a propane-fueled cooking stove and refrigerator/freezer.

We left the open waters, rounded an island, and the green lodge and red boathouse came into sight. I throttled back the motor and let the wind carry us to the dock. The sound of the trailing boat wake lapped along the rocky shore, echoing through the air.

With the boat secured, we headed up the trail to the lodge with our, hopefully, still-frozen delight. We went inside to the waiting fridge and deposited the ice cream into the ice-encrusted freezer compartment. With our mission successfully completed, it was now time to make the chocolaty hot fudge sauce.

Where the recipe originated, I'm not sure. It was in my mom's recipe file on a three-by-five card that was stained with decades of spills from the recipe's ingredients. Already, I had been cooking the sauce for years, and the ingredients and cooking directions were burned

3

into my memory. The hot fudge sauce, a mixture of butter, sugar, baker's chocolate, salt, vanilla extract, and evaporated milk, was cooked to just below boiling. As it cooked, a chocolaty aroma filled the kitchen air, pushing against the smell of the towering pine forest outside.

Tonight, it was the guests' turn to prepare the evening meal. I don't remember what my mom cooked up, as it was so many years ago. I will, however, never forget the hot fudge sauce I made and poured over the dishes filled with vanilla ice cream.

Soon the dinner bell rang, and we all gathered around the long wood table in the lodge dining room, enjoying company and the meal.

After a short break from dinner, we all took our seats again and dug into the sweet concoction placed before us. The only sound: spoons scooping up the delicious treat. With the treat complete, silence was replaced by conversation of memories past, joys of the present, and adventures waiting in the future.

Nightfall was fast approaching. The once blue sky was now painted a pinkish red. It was time—time to light the Coleman lanterns. We lit the lanterns to a chorus of crying loons. The glowing lanterns' light filled the room and flickered on the rustic walls and the moose head above the stone fireplace, bringing the old bull to life. The lanterns had a distinct hissing sound to them; it was a mesmerizing, calming sound.

Well, it was getting quite late now, and we were all tired from the day's activities. Everyone said good night, and I headed off to my room with lantern in hand. I placed my lantern on the table next to the bed and crawled between the flannel sheets. I reached over, turned the fuel knob to off, and listened to the hissing subside. The light slowly faded as the lantern burned off the remaining fuel. It was now pitch black, and I quickly fell asleep.

Even today, with so many years past, I can hear the hiss of that lantern, see the glow of its light, and taste that hot fudge over ice cream from the boat run called the Kakagi ice cream express.

KAKAGI HOT FUDGE SAUCE

½ Cup Butter

4 Squares Baking Chocolate 3 Cups Sugar

1 Can Evaporated Milk 1 Teaspoon Vanilla

½ Teaspoon Salt

Melt butter and baking chocolate in saucepan over low heat. Once melted and mixed remove from heat.

Add the sugar to the melted ingredients.

Now slowly stir in the evaporated milk and heat slowly to just about boiling.

Stir continuously to keep it from burning. While heating the sauce add salt and vanilla.

Once heated remove from burner and enjoy over your favorite ice cream.

The Swim

William D. Van Atta Jr.

The crowd chanted, "5, 4, 3, 2, 1!" The air horn blasted, and I advanced in a wave of swimmers across the beach and into the frigid, clear waters of Lake Superior. The shock of the icy water felt like pins and needles on the bare skin not protected by the wetsuit.

As a kid, I remember playing with my brothers and sisters in the waters at Washburn City Campground, just south of Bayfield Wisconsin. We would jump off the end of the dock and race back. Your body would be numb by the time you reached shore. We would shiver, laugh, run to the dock's end, and do it again.

I took a few strokes, then slowly settled into a rhythm. Feeling a bit anxious, I collided with several swimmers on my way to the float marking the first turn. My brain generated thoughts: Why are you doing this? Just turn around and get out.

I kept going, rounded the first marker, and entered the open water. This was my fourth year taking part in the Bayfield, Point to La Pointe event. It began in Bayfield and finished at Madeline, one of the Apostle Islands a distance of 2.1 miles.

This year, my sister Sylvia and Brothers Tim and Tom joined me, along with about 600 others. As I stroked along, thoughts about my life took me back to where my love affair with water began.

My first memory of swimming was when I was four years old, taking lessons. My dad was an elementary school physical education teacher, and one of his many specialties was aquatics. He taught me how to swim, giving me this wonderful lifetime gift.

My skills developed quickly, and by age seven, I was competing as a member of the team my dad started—University Swim Club. We worked out year-round in the 20-yard pool at the Old Armory on the campus of the University of Iowa. We always parked in the gravel lot behind The Old Armory, then walked around the building and entered the pool through a side door. You had to ascend a few steps to get to the pool.

On the wall to the left of the doorway hung a gas mask next to some large yellow cylinders labeled CHLORINE GAS. Further to the left was the room that housed the water filter system for the pool. I am not sure who handled pool maintenance, but the water was always warm and clear. However, it was probably over-chlorinated. The exposure bleached our Speedos yes, I am a recovering Speedo wearer. It also lightened and shined our hair, and because we did not wear goggles, our eyes would burn.

Not only did our eyes burn, but our sight became foggy, and psychedelic yellow-green halos appeared around bright objects. Although the water was clear and clean, this was not the case for the pool bottom. There was a collection of debris scattered in the depths. It was a conglomeration of dirt, clumps of hair, an occasional Band-Aid, and rare treasures of coins and jewelry.

Before my dad let us kids into the pool, he would go inside and make a quick check for the presence of others. Occasionally, he would forget to check, and we would be exposed to a naked Dr. Oppenheimer. He was a professor who usually swam before our practice began. He swam by himself in the buff. It was more than once that we saw his skinny, naked body rinsing off in the poolside showers. This time, my dad checked, and all was clear.

There were a couple of locker rooms and a small office in the facility. On a bulletin board by the office window that opened to the pool was a poem on a well-worn sheet of yellowing paper. We often would read it and laugh. It still holds true and makes me chuckle when I read it.

The Swimming Pool

Tony Lerma

The swimming pool is deep and cold.
The gutters are filled with spit and mold.
The smell on the benches is really neat,
It smells like the scum on a dead man's feet.

The chlorine in the pool is really swell.
If it gets in your eyes, it burns like hell.
It makes no difference if you're fat or thin
If you swim in chlorine, it'll rot your skin.

"First group up!" is the famous cry.
It makes you wanna stop and die.
Fifty-eight hundreds will be our fate,
So we might be out by half past eight.

"Five more to go," and the feeling's fine,
But look at the clock it's half past nine.
Practice is over "Yeah baby, cool,"
At least we're free from the swimming pool.

The
Swimming Pool

The swimming pool is deep and
cold,
The gutters are filled with spit
and mold.
The smell on the benches is really
neat,
It smells like the scum on a dead
man's feet.
The chlorine in the pool is really
swell,
If it gets in your eyes it burns
like hell.
It makes no difference if you're
fat or thin,
If you swim in chlorine it'll rot
your skin.
"First group up!" is the famous cry,
It makes you wana stop and die,
Fifty-eight hundreds will be our
fate,
So we might be out by half past.

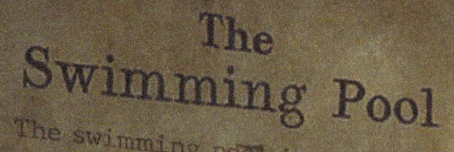

I was about a half mile out and still a little bit anxious, almost panicky. I stopped, did a few breaststrokes, and then sensed a swimmer to my left. I raised my head and looked in that direction. I recognized the stroke. It was Sylvia! She put her head up and asked how I was doing. I told her, not too well, but that I should be able to make it. I had been plagued with anxiety since my time in the Army, and recently it was surfacing during open water swims. Most of the time, I was able to work through it. She gave me some encouragement, then swam on ahead. I took a few more resting strokes, adjusted my "The Magic5" custom-fitted goggles, and then continued toward the island.

I remember the day Dad introduced us to goggles. They were blue, crude, and bulky. It took a lot of adjusting to get a good fit. They were very prone to leaking and left marks on your face from the tight strap. Out of the water, the field of view was restricted; submerged, it was even worse. The light refracted differently underwater, making your vision double, like looking cross-eyed. This took some getting used to. They did offer protection from the harsh chlorine. We only used them for workouts. They were not good enough to wear in competition. It would be a couple more years before we could wear goggles in meets.

I celebrated my seventh birthday and soon after swam in my first meet. It took place in Moline, Illinois. I competed in several events in the 8-and-under age group. I placed sixth in one event and received my first award a pink ribbon. I was not happy about my performance or the pink ribbon and was determined to do better next time.

As best I recall, we competed in meets every couple of weeks that summer. By season's end, I had accumulated a few trophies, medals, and several ribbons. I neatly displayed them with that first pink ribbon on a shelf above the radiator in my room.

I recall one meet at the Iowa City Recreation Center when a fellow competitor got sick on me as we were being marshaled into heats. I was rushed to the shower where I rinsed off, then ran to make it just in time for my swim.

A couple of years went by. I was becoming a well-rounded swimmer. I excelled most in the longer-distance freestyle events. During this period, my dad completed his dissertation and was awarded a PhD. From that point on, he was Dr. Van Atta, but everyone soon referred to him as "Doc."

Fourth grade was my last year attending University Elementary School in Iowa City. My dad accepted a position as a professor in Physical Education at the University of Wisconsin–La Crosse (UW-L). We spent a lot of the summer shuttling household items to La Crosse. I made several trips in the old green bus my dad was converting to a camper.

My family was large seven kids, four boys and three girls so we had a lot to move. It was a four-hour journey to La Crosse, and without a new home, we put everything we could into storage. The storage building was a former funeral home. It was dark and creepy. There were items like embalming equipment and an old casket lid that had been left behind.

Across the street was Henry's, 15-Cent Hamburgers. I spent a lot of spare change there over the years.

I was starting to feel more comfortable and picked up the pace. I lifted my head every few strokes to make sure I was on course. If you strayed, you were met by a safety kayaker and redirected. I passed the orange halfway marker and could easily see where the finish line was. It was marked by a large smoke fire that was clearly visible.

Summer was over. We settled into our new home in La Crosse and started at a new school Campus School at the University of Wisconsin–La Crosse. It was my first day as a fifth grader. My dad escorted me to the classroom, where I was welcomed by Mrs. Johnson and several students. I was shown my desk, and the school year was off to a start.

There was no formal swimming team for kids in La Crosse, but I soon learned about a small group of boys who worked out at the YMCA. The building was built in 1909, and it had a 15-yard pool in the basement. It was crowded and chaotic trying to swim in the small pool.

My dad soon became involved, and with his expertise, things became more organized. The girls had a similar situation they swam in the indoor pool at the Bluff View Motel. To supplement our training, we would swim at the university with my dad in one of Wittich Hall's 20-yard pools.

A new YM/YWCA was soon under construction. It included a beautiful 25-yard, 6-lane pool. The new pool soon became home to the La Crosse Y Swim Team. My dad was head coach. He was helped by several assistant coaches and dedicated parents.

In the summer, we would use the city's Erickson and Memorial pools. These pools were not heated, and they remained icy cold through most of the summer. We swam in the early morning, and by the time the workout was over, your teeth chattered and your frozen body shook uncontrollably.

I swam on. The water was calm and flat, with just a light breeze. There was an occasional wave, probably coming from the Madeline Island Ferry operating just south of the course. I was hit by a wave as I was taking a breath and took in a mouthful of water. I had to stop to clear my airway and catch my breath. I started back up and headed for the finish line. I thought, no guts, no glory.

The sign on the locker room wall in Wittich Hall read in bold black letters, "No Guts, No Glory." I glanced up at it, then headed upstairs to the pool. I was training for the Quincy YMCA Swim Marathon with my dad and sisters, Molly and Sylvia. The swim covered a 10-mile stretch of the Mississippi from La Grange, Missouri, to Quincy, Illinois. We trained every day, sometimes twice. I would occasionally get painful cramps in my legs and would be forced to take a break.

It was time. We rode the old green bus to Quincy and spent the night crowded into a Holiday Inn. For our race day breakfast, my dad insisted that we have steak and eggs. We were shuttled to the start area, where we put on our suits and lathered on some baking grease for insulation. Then, sequenced one after another, we entered the muddy Mississippi and began our swim downstream.

Each swimmer had a safety boat with a driver and a lookout. My lookout was one of my school friends. The river was near flood stage with a strong current, so the race times were fast. I think most completed the swim in less than two hours. That was the second time I did the swim and the last. The event was not held after that.

I did swim in the Black River swim that was held one year. It was five miles, running from the Airport Beach on French Island to the Big Indian at Riverside Park in La Crosse. I did not swim in any more marathons after that but continued to concentrate on the distance events. I stayed on the Y team through high school. There was no high school swim team or a pool. I did run some cross country and track, but by my junior year, I gave it up for swimming.

A pair of inverted kicking feet suddenly appeared in front of me. Fortunately, I stopped quickly enough to avoid a kick to the face. As I stopped and raised my head, cramps attacked my legs. I found myself facing a young woman doing elementary backstroke. She was in a little distress and said she was seasick. I told her I had leg cramps, then moved on. I was able to change my stroke to lessen the pain. The cramps subsided, and I picked up the pace. I was feeling tired but good. I could clearly see the smoke and people near the finish. The adrenaline was kicking in.

My signature event: the 1650 nearly a mile in a 25-yard pool. I was a college sophomore at UW–L, swimming in the Wisconsin State University Conference Championships. I was about 1,000 yards into the race and not far from the lead swimmers. I hit my turn perfectly, came off the wall, and was consumed by a surge of energy. It was like a switch was flipped. I scanned my competitors and, to my surprise, saw that I was in front. I felt no pain and stroked away effortlessly. I could see my teammates running along the poolside, cheering me on. The lap gun fired two lengths to go. I felt goosebumps all the way to the finish. I touched the wall. I was conference champion.

That was my best performance ever. The summer after my victory, I trained at the University of Iowa's Intensive Swim Camp. Swimmers of all ages trained there, including an Australian Olympian. We swam three workouts a day, averaging 15 to 18 thousand yards daily. Eat, sleep, swim, and repeat. I was in the best condition of my life, but my junior and senior years were plagued by illness, burnout, and great disappointment.

I graduated from college, went into the Army, and took up running. When I was deployed to Saudi Arabia in support of Desert Shield and then Desert Storm, I decided to try a little swimming to supplement my running. I swam in the small pool at the compound where I stayed.

Soon I was relocated to King Khalid Military City (KKMC), in the middle of the desert. The city was very ornate, with gardens and fountains. It reminded me of the Emerald City from *The Wizard of Oz*. I was able to find an unused 50-meter indoor pool in the heart of the city. I swam there a few times before the war started and shut the facility down.

One afternoon, I entered the pool, and behind me, two heavily armed soldiers appeared. They checked the area, then a man emerged in a swimsuit. I recognized him as one of the generals we regularly flew, Lieutenant General Pagonis. I completed my swim in the presence of the general and his bodyguards, then returned to my quarters to await the next mission.

I left the Army and started swimming regularly again when a fitness center opened in the community where I lived. I have continued to swim since then, taking the gift with me wherever I go.

Just a few hundred yards to go I could smell the smoke from the signal fire. I could hear music and the PA announcing the finishing participants. The sandy bottom came into view. I rounded the final marker and fell in line behind some other finishers. I climbed up the exit stairs and staggered across the finish line. I smiled and sighed in relief.

I changed out of my wetsuit, then joined family and friends. We reminisced about our past swimming experiences and gave credit to all who had helped us along the way. Then we made our way to the ferry that would take us back to where the adventure began.

I stood at the shore, looked back at Madeline Island, and with a grin thought that, just like the swim, life wasn't about winning a pink ribbon, a medal, not even a trophy but about the journey and sharing it with family and friends.

"Keep Swimming! "

Poems

WINTER WIND

The wind, the wind, the wind it blows

It blows and blows, it blows so cold

It grasps you with its ice chilled hands

And carries you off to warmer lands

The wind, the wind, the wind it blows

MY FRIEND

The wind is my friend, the wind it is.

It raps at my window, it knocks at my door,

It whistles and whines through the cracks in my floor.

And when the skies are clear and the nights are cold

It howls above the sounds of the fire's hot coals.

It is outside and I within, and the wind it tries to find its way in.

Shall I open my door and let it in?

MARIAH'S SONG

Oh sweet Mariah, blaze a trail to a life far beyond this earth

To a paradise in the mountains where the streams run cool and pure Where gentle breezes blow in your face carrying enticing smells

And the sky, it's a cobalt blue with fluffy clouds of white

In the dark of night the stars and moon shine bright while the northern lights dance about

And there you'll howl those ancient tunes that echo through the night

As you run that trail look back for us, for we are not too far behind

But until then you'll run in our hearts where your memories are sacred, happy and dear

My Old Friend

My old friend came to see me today, showed up uninvited, that's usually the way

Triggered by a smell, word, sight or sound something I said something I found.

My old friend took me to a dark empty space. I've been here before It's a lonely place.

There I cover and hide my face. Perhaps this is where I'll meet my fate?

My old friend came to see me today.

I wish my old friend would stay away.

RIVERS

Rivers, rivers, rivers flow

Some are high and some are low

Some are fast and some are slow

In spite of all the things I know

I still am wondering

Where they go

NORTHERN LIGHTS

The northern lights came out last night

Oh yes! And they greeted me

As I looked down on the mirrored lake

They looked up at me

TIME

Time passes it ticks away.

I try to stop it, but it flies away.

I try to slow it but older I grow.

And when I am bored with nothing to do, the hands of the clock, they no longer move.

Time passes it ticks away.

CRY AND PRAY

I've been lonely since you've gone. Nothing seems to ease the pain.

I cry and pray and think of you and wish our lives could be renewed.

But I know that will not take place, so I cry and pray in this lonely place.

The nights, they are the worst for me, the darkness holds no sympathy.

So, I cry and pray. I fall asleep, then wake again to a lonely day.

SOMEWHERE

Some where there is a valley with a river running wide and deep.

Its banks are lined with bluffs, with sides that are so steep.

Down in this valley, the trees are always green.

And the sweet smell of wildflowers makes the air smell, so fresh and clean.

The wind there it blows gently, there are no violent storms.

And there, my little Mitzy, roams free, for evermore.

NIGHT FALL

The woods are quiet now

The wind it slowly dies

And the skies grow darker

Now giving way to the clearness of night

In the distance a loon can be heard

She sends her eerie cry across the glassy waters

To my shore nearby

And the sun

It releases its lasts rays

They dance and then die on the large pine trunks towering overhead

Then all, all is in darkness